MALCONTENTS

To Mary

(NEAB for 1996?)

Love,

John Forth

March '94.

John Forth

MALCONTENTS

Rockingham Press

Published in 1994
by
The Rockingham Press
11 Musley Lane,
Ware, Herts
SG12 7EN

British Library Cataloguing-in-Publication Data

A catalogue record for this book
is available from the British Library

ISBN 1 873468 22 9

Printed in Great Britain
by Bemrose Shafron (Printers) Ltd,
Chester

Printed on Recycled Paper

Eastern Arts Board Funded

For Bill and Rose Forth

ACKNOWLEDGEMENTS

Acknowledgements are due to the following publications in which some of these poems first appeared:
The London Magazine, Poetry Durham, Outposts, Verse, Owl, A Sense of Place (East Midlands Arts), *Envoi, The North, New Prospects*, and *Spoils* (Poetry Business 1991).

CONTENTS

IN THE FRAME

A year before we met and ten before
our firstborn, she went quietly.

We count our blessings in a house
no bigger, less earthy, than hers.

She would have honoured her pledge
to come but wouldn't have been

at home here, knowing how her great
grandgirls barely tolerate townies.

One's reading in a hammock, strung
near the top of the silver birch,

but if she grasps the hook and pulley
and takes her death-slide down

she'll pass over the other one hanging
like a bat from the monkey-frame.

We're just inside the hundred mile
limit she kept on seaside trains

for one-day holidays, and if I listen
carefully I know what she'd say.

Go and see what them bleedin' kids
are doing and tell 'em to stop it.

VACUEES

With an ear to the sky's pregnant drone,
she waved him off to the mines
where he cranked his way down

to the face before dawn in a cage,
and darkness turned to day
in the space between landings.

She was ready to skip through the war
out of ear-shot and marry young,
and though talking was a damp squib,

she'd recreate her fears of doodlebugs
for boys who skinned live mice
in their teeth and hung the hides to dry.

Later he would freeze behind new curtains,
cheating death by recalling
the population of whole streets gone.

Before they'd consider the post-war boom
and life's possibility, various
holes needed blowing underground.

AN AWKWARD AGE

The door of St. James's made it too easy
to score, and games were discouraged
anyway with gestures from inside.
The woodshed gate was best to defend.

When a day's flag and ritual had ended
we boo-hooed into salad for the Queen
and collected a golden coach and four
with new sovereigns to mark the time.

You might run away from Sunday School
but not a Coronation. Leaving early
added to the cost, like smiling
shame-facedly at the prim figures

mother's friends had crossed themselves
before, inexplicably. Icons, mementos,
food for the grand occasion; even
the blessed money I managed to lose.

SOLDIER BOYS

The rain smudges our grey terrace,
keeping us all in and occupied.
We've heard the surrounding streets
are being laid waste by morning
and we talk ourselves into sharing
uneasy calm. Houses from each end
will shift and crumble into the alleys,
then close up like a spacious gum.

Our tale earns twelve hours' grace
by giving the past a tacit feel
and leaving a few still standing.
Even stumbling out into something
well-short of a new armageddon
hardly matters. We'll huddle
in the concrete shelter and turn
the bomb-site over, looking for sun.

COLD WAR

Annihilated by her long silence
we'd never outface mother,
tight as a gunman who knew
how little she needed to do.

The radio's urgent background
drew us in, confirming
the old fears. When several
destroyers droned in on Cuba

our wars and small-time passions
were a betrayal. Anyone young
or asleep might never guess
fire was a fire from the noise.

She would find us whispering,
watching out the daylight
in compliance. No singeing
could immunise against the hurt.

THE KNOWLEDGE

Politely nurtured reproduction frames
outstripped ordinary hours,
and she would nag him repeatedly
about the consequence of care.

He thought he might try mugging up
streets for gentler redeployment,
calling-over each run meticulously
until he could walk her there.

He let the whole place unravel itself
while she totted up the profits,
using the flexible wage to fill up
the house like an Antique Fair,

but soon the hours would cost him
more than either job was worth,
exposing his way of handling a cab
as if it were the perfect chair.

TRIKE

We stripped my earliest transport of its white
diagonal flash from the front-plate
and tightened the chain to enhance power.
I was late mastering the real thing
but kept ahead by developing unreal speeds
on the downhill roll. I'd do the block
in three minutes and turn on a sixpence.

Although its ornate red mudguards stood out
in a race my credibility rested
on the simulated *clun*k of doors slamming
whenever I parked in the kerb.
It was bought at the time when everyone
was into two-wheelers, and crushed
when a black Hillman reversed like a train.

DEATH IN THE FAMILY

The Ottawa 236, a big shadowy
upright against her wall,
forbidden like us to make
any racket or be party to one.

Older model with the over-damper.
It cost her sixty pounds-seven
and-six in quarterly chunks.
Thirty-one guineas new in '31

she couldn't do, but snapped it up
second hand, still clean in '43
for us to shake our sticks at.
She never played or polished it

but guarded it to the war's end,
along with bills and letters
chucked away when she died:
On looking over your piano

the manager considers that there is
no actual damage done
to the piano, that could be claimed for
through the War Damage.

Before the piano is delivered to you
again we will clean it out
and revive the polish work
ourselves also tune same.

The same binge had left her
nurturing a modish three-piece
with matching coverlets,
an overpowering sideboard

and a new cylindrical hoover
that still made convincing noises
when we cleared the place out.
The piano was for Albert,

who couldn't play and didn't
make it back from Burma.
When the dealer came nearly fifty
years of relative silence later,

he opened it up, looked in, shook
his head and made as if to
frown a few times before saying
he'd been hoping for a 238,

so we checked the old paper work,
weighed him up against council
rates and a bid from her next door
and knocked seven-and-six off.

TRANSATLANTIC

We couldn't believe our American cousin,
leaning in too close above Pinky's
tank and stirring the mush with a pencil.

The two families rode all his breaking-in
on conversations: ours speechless,
his modern, or almost cajoling

when he stood in the doorway waving our fish
as if he'd never seen one. We didn't
rush him, but patiently nursed it back, then

Look at little fishy swimmin' aroun' in the water
he called to Norma, his ex-pat mum
and a gathering of Kirks and Dirks immersed

in the long tale of how much better life was
in colour, while Benny Goodman
played on the new hire-purchase stereo-gram

you couldn't buy any more over there.
That fish was aeons old, had more than survived
its seven-day wonderful partner, Perky,

and the heady atmosphere five floors up
in our London block, but it grew transparent
within a week and died. I watched him

like a security guard for the rest of his stay,
dangerous though quite unarmed, trying
to come to terms with where he'd come from.

THE FIFTIES

Nearly anyone pushing fifty at the millennium
will have seen Moby Dick's bellyful
of Rolls Royce engines hit the bottom,
and wept as Ahab went down with the cars.

Some still won't have shaken off that tune
the Stargazers sang about over the mountains
and longing to be, thinking they still see
the sea from the side as we think we did then.

It was White and Blanchflower before the storm,
when Trad was servicemen two doors along
and the buses were electric more or less
and the Comet was only a crowd-pulling jet

and none knew the war except on a screen
that was taken away before their birth
and filled again. Many will say they ran
from jelly-fish without being stung.

But a few too many saw Disney's lemmings
pouring in thousands over the edge
at a tender age, and spent their lives
wondering why the cameraman didn't stop it.

SELECTED ROUTES

You can't accelerate going in or out.
A winding street and children's
yelling place in half-light,
with people so close you could hear
a cough in the night or share
nestlings with a neighbour's cat.

Who'd care now for blackout rations
or the noise of an outdoor flush,
for days when every boy came over
awkward and the girls were Rose.

*

A raftered roof incongruously spread
above an explosion of cut flowers
and ornate lamps, a neater century's
wooden finish imperfectly stained...

The Romantic, rekindled, as always
draws a crowd. With barely seconds to go
we shimmy into an empty pew
but the quartet's only talking tactics.

They seem intrigued by the quick jazz
of a horse clopping by in the dark.

*

The last remaining street looks planned now,
still boasting the odd Victorian feature
and chilly inconvenience but receding
with the shutters closed. The old names
have been lifted over and hammered in again,
braced on new pillars in a gilded scrawl.

Too young to be in there at the death
we couldn't sustain its walking pace.
Calling in time to pay ourselves a visit,
we leave at thirty sure of losing the way.

T.S. ELIOT ON CASSETTE

The Wasteland's mainly conjuring
trams, not ceremony or kings.
It makes me think of a pub
by the Thames drowned in sepia

or the model town I played in,
its muddle of desert-rats
and pre-war cars showing
their teeth in chaotic jams.

Being shunted across it to see
my dad come home in uniform's
caught now like a still frame.
Driving a Six-five-three down

from Whitechapel to The Green
and hooking-up in full view
was heroism. The TV cop's
frown came with the badge.

High-tec fuses then with after
like an elegant shirt
and everything's reduced
to new metaphors in a box,

but this one sounds like a second
airing of Edwardian styles,
most of recorded history
being ransacked for photos.

The clanking and jarring's gone
but the stair still sways:
hi-fi's no-hiss pressed
into three-speed monochrome.

MALCONTENTS

A Public Appearance

The doctors have insisted nothing's wrong
but I'm sobbing us all to sleep,
hungering after everything
and yelling till mother cracks.

My good for nothing deluge leaves her
floundering in worse tears
than Grandad's cancer, caused,
they say, by a rotten lung.
Sure as God's in 'ell he'd have loved yer!
they told me often later.

When they carry me down to the bed
I'm still blorting. *The little bleeder's
got more 'air than me already,*
he says, clearly warmed by the blast.

Players

Sinfield wasn't no common name
so they claimed he wasn't much worse
than he ought to have been,
that he 'ad 'is work cut out
keeping 'er in 'and, that maybe
we was all entitled to be thankful
he turned out equal to the part.

He got through fifty or sixty fags
a day and still found time
to load a crane till it nudged him
into bed. I tried to picture
the type of crane, and the cards
he must have stashed away somewhere,
but none ever came to light.

Gambler

She spent her Saturdays with race-cards,
cursing form, and often came back
staggering in the dark at seventy —
a night of crooning rounded off —
with brandy, *easier on the 'art.*

After pressing untold riches into a sash
under her skirt, she'd tell me
the banks, like Piggot, Churchill
and *orse-piddles* would let her down.

The unfamiliar loosened belt struck home
like a cancelled meeting or a song
past time, or as if some bastard
favourite's failure to finish strong
could be forgotten by morning.

Family Tree

Four years old among midday traffic
I try to shout above the bells
and a man swings yelling at cars.

When the engines drift back empty
my dad draws long on his pipe
and tells me they're going for coal.

Maybe Tarzan'll rescue the cinders
from a pile of ash, but heat
spreads easy as falling off a tree

and what if all this burning crackles
endlessly? No use pretending
we'll smoulder on a bit longer.

I'm wondering whose fear of flames
those men'll be stoking next time.

Malcontents

One by one her regular friends in age
had each upturned a greenish
dome-like belly towards the ceiling
and broken a bond. Then to meet a man
to share the nightly sips of stout
and awkward sociable pecking
helped clear the air — but afterwards,
with the room in a tighter corner,
her run-down cage would rattle
with foreign birds: three of those
new bright-feathered nipping types
who squeaked as if in pain
or in want of singing, their colours
more unsettling than a ritual bell.

Market

Nigel Henderson,
Photographs of Bethnal Green.

Down the Lane you could buy stuffed owls
and a kind of paradise in stamps.
Eggs and feathers lay in sawdust under glass.
The place looked hard to handle.

Streets would unwind irritably through backyards
full of ghosts and bricked-in roses,
little theatres frozen with their signs:
Bagwash and Knife-Grinder, Stockings, Prize Beer.

The snaps are a giveaway but it can take an age
to master a salesman's patter,
even if you admire his tiptoe poise.

Straight off the peg and dressed to kill,
we shuffle by with houses on our backs,
hanging a strained face on every stall.

Collector

When my costly brother was blooded
hardly anyone kicked or cried
but I had a new Spitfire for my pains.
It was the first in a line of toys
bought to counter-balance fear:
cars and planes for operations,
soldiers for colds and tooth-repair.

I'd learn to ignore the momentary flame
and nearly any brief promise,
but most collections still pack more
wallop at the start — when trying
not to begin seems hardly worth the pain
of relative costing, and the kick
inside carries no particular reward.

Late Victorians

Trim as a corporal, he'd given up hours
to muvver's dirt, miles from anywhere
and deep as hell, simmering till dusk
when she'd be waiting by the back door
to watch him drag home sacks like corpses.
He'd have taken down his strap to us,
she said, if he'd had any puff left in him.

His cow-son of a son held out for the lot
but she managed to save the old last
with two bronzes and a fading *Ben Hur*
he'd never miss. She'd scrawled her own
dedication inside. The wrangling left her
breathless, looking her age, knowing
he'd coughed up pounds for his reading.

Soap

Looking too sad to be saved, a cherub
pissed on the graveyard,
the boy who died refusing to piddle
or unable to. Pure cussedness
either way but it made me
wet the wall behind her house all day
to keep my insides sluiced.

Her chiselled block of red *Carbolic*
stung far more than green *Fairy*.
Luckily she had no bath.
Caught between my devilry and the sea,
she was water-tight as anything
God offered: *You do as I say,*
or I'll come straight back 'n haunt yer!

Friends and Neighbours

Disconnected but still burning, I recreate
the spread of a Blitz blaze in electric
storms and shut out school for the day.
Although I've composed a swirling octopus
drowned in green and water-smeared
I'm inconsolable. At home later
my tea looks blurred and comfortless,
the one-off tricks of lightning
strain credibility and the wireless
fizzes and peters out. Everyone begs me
to see how fighting a fire can be easy
but I'm gone to earth and smothered,
shaking like a flame. I'll never escape
the song that's seeping back to me.

Germs

Mother's all-but-clinical fear was nurtured
in both her sons. Every grating
was given a widening berth
as we conjured *Boys' Own* enemies
squatting like gargoyles in the drains.

Comparing our paltry intake of dirt
with her own *friggin' bushels,*
Nan reckoned the odds on a table
spread with yesterday's slop-stained *Racing
Tips* and carefully vetted the sums.

You 'n yer silliness'll drive me under
she'd say, as we sat by the fire
disinfected, trying to move
our troops across a tray of mould.

Ear, Nose and Throat

Stuck in a busy ward for specialists
I'm gripped by each film,
but the ones for children help my wars
flare on — *Silver Sword* or *Jesus*
serialised in weekly parts.
Fortitude's no comfort on a screen.

I'm pleading to hear their letters again
but I can read them perfectly well
myself the frazzled matron says;
a dozen kids are less trouble than me.

Mad as a tank in bandage, one of them escapes
smelling of struggle — and we're left
with a clock's buzzing for company,
*Atishoo*ing too loudly for *All Fall Down*.

Wheels and Deals

I can just remember the bus whirring
and jarring beneath electric wires,
the conductor winking at me
as he waved aside my mum's coin,
and dad frowning at the wheel
while she sat clutching her secret profit
all the way home. I'd forgotten
my stumbling in the downstairs aisle
and huddling by the safety-rail
with him in the cabin staring straight ahead;
the way she'd smile and pat her purse,
intent on keeping us all in sway.
Yet nowadays whenever I ride
on buses I fumble and usually pay.

Remembrance

On the eleventh day of the eleventh month,
Susan Bowles and I would be looking
guiltily up at the plaque on the wall
and pretending not to be touching arms
under thick coats or wondering
what the fuss was about. She was a fast
runner and could beat several boys
at chess, but she lived at the darker end,
her grey PT vests and rakish laughter
enough to make my mother ask if I wanted
to play with her again. If I'd had my way
I would have done, but at the ripening
of eleven I went off to the all-boys'
school and she went off with the boys.

Carrier

She'd been hurried away to the sticks
with her own blitz in a bag,
one of a crowd of kids steaming out
when Warsaw blew. She remembers
diphtheria, the twisted faces caught
and wheeled away like soldiers,
her sister's punishing grin.

You can see the whole family twitch
when the temperature's high
but it's love she sets her table for,
her fear of immunity's power
sharp as a film. She still squirms
at news-footage and the blow
she hopes she never delivered me.

Street Fire

On a wicked night we gather in pyjamas
to watch the woodyard dissolve
in a ruffled sky. Stiff planks had blazed
into my sleep and crackled overhead,
coming to life in a muddle of war
and witches whacking the air with brooms.
Real fires never smoulder;
they offer escapes that outrun fear.

Standing too close I imagine the whole
bewildered circle burning and learn
how easy it is to smother heat.
Alive, abandoned, out of bed and drawn
to the space we'll claim tomorrow,
I never once see myself in the flames.

LEARNING FROM NATURE

For if he or we could see better
we would know, but we have to go on.
(Richard Eberhart)

Flushing the pint-sized pond
uncovered a mud-dweller, skulking
two and a half feet in the dark
below lilies, its feelers
barely pulsating. Goldfish,
grown too old for the light,
slithered over new-mown grass
where birds were bathing.

It's sunset and a pigeon has spent
its clearly audible weight
on the plate glass door, needing
ninety seconds' ambiguous gasping
to die. Call it irrationality,
this relief when he goes unaided,
my conviction he wanted only

the one good eye to picture the rest
instead of lying transfixed
in a wide-beaked gaze,
apparently broken by air.

BAT IN AUTUMN

Glazed in the half-light,
trudging home,
we stopped at a muddy church
where voices boomed
in shy whispers.

There it was, unfurling itself
slowly on the flags,
just breathing, teasing us
with one eye open
and staring us down.

We brought it outside for air
but it froze, crouched
seething on a grave, withdrawing
its rat-head to a point
and squinting at the stones.

We could feel the body quicken
before it disappeared
in a shelter of wings,
setting the heart for quiet.
Someone said it needed a longer

drop for its flight so we left it
perched firmly on a log
wedged between a drainpipe
and the wall and waited
for a last flutter into the dark.

Far too tired even for sleep,
it saw us watching.
We gathered up the coat
we'd used as a cradle,
joked about a good innings

and how much better off
it might have been
left inside, promised ourselves
the visit tomorrow
we guessed we'd forget.

IMMERSION

I find *The Brighton Municipal*'s hot water
barely warm but it's one of those days
with a future. The pure in heart can sense
possibilities in love, new directions.
I book my bath but can't find the porter
anywhere, and then in strolls this man

with a mission and suddenly it's every man
for himself. I settle back in the water,
gently rippling, hoping eventually the porter
would hear and thinking several days
of archaeology might reveal the direction
I've taken. He'd hardly need a sixth sense.

You were lukewarm too, I remember. No sense
of timing................ Anyway this man
bursts in, makes a bee-line in the direction
of the best bath and demands hot water.
You legal, he shouts, *I never get me days
right with this place.* The missing porter

scurries along in his wake as any porter
would. *Large or small,* he says, maybe sensing
no workaday wash, the whole day's
business in one. *Depends,* says the man,
but usually small when I'm under water.
He laughs and then asks for directions

to the mortuary, has had clear directions
to them all except Brighton. The porter
finally thinks to send me some water
but all at once, and colder than refined sense
can bear. *If it's near a station,* the man
calls out, *I can do 'em all in a day....*

but I'm not fussed. Most I do these days
use 'ospitals, so give me directions
there if you're stuck. I wonder which man
will crack first: the worried porter
wanting his old job back, me with a sense
of injustice or the ghoul. *Is that water*

hot enough, is meant for me, but cold water
dampens more than a wish or two after days
of uncertainty, and anyway I can sense
the feeling coming back. I need a direction
but not the kind offered by the porter.
You know me, quick in / out, says the man.

None of my plans hold water; the old man's
make sense, but knowing the direction's not all.
The porter has scrubbed out far better days.

SCRAPS

The poor old sod (at ninety-
odd in dog years) sleeps
and slops no more, his place
downstairs reverting back

to whatever it was, and there's
nothing quite as nullifying
as seeing him finally gone out.
It's also pointless denying

he knew what death was about.
Good at the hasty burial,
childhood sweet and sharer
of old meat or homes,

he was thrown bits of reverence
no elegy gets in the end.
He bowed out knowing the price
of maturity in his bones.

YOUNG MUSICIAN OF THE YEAR

If one so young can take by the hand
the dying Elgar in his despair
and walk him gently through
then it's true, there must be
something new in the affair.

Her critics were earnestly offering
thoughts of developing cutting
edge and a kind of instinct
although she probably couldn't hear.

Her hands tight with a new passion,
she wipes one on her bright dress
to remind us that nothing done well
is made to measure — one moment's
abandon cutting out the entire hall.

COLLEGE BOY

You can't raise a Kane back up
when he's in defeat. (J.R. Robertson)

i.m. Steve W.

Late for a drink but always drunk
and broke for love or money,
you'd sing and remain untouched
by audience, entertaining girls
you were too scared to meet.

Appearing so often at wrong times
that all times appeared wrong,
you were close to the edge
with a mixture of wild affection
that could empty rooms.

One day in a blight of sizzling
heat stays. Another visit,
you in a frenzy halving an army
of wasps with a steel comb
as if you were celebrating.

You couldn't get yourself back
in defeat, driving old Dixie
down where no bells rang.
After a night of bad singing
you drank up and left us behind.

NARROW DEFEAT

Better get this job over quick. Listen....
(James Joyce — Ulysses)

It was you or Spurs I seem to remember
but the climate's usual turn for the worse
decided it. You'd washed and dressed
in a field, and were in no mood to swallow
a full dose of mud-soaked football.

I drove in silence, wrestling with the ghost
of a poem and the title race, but intent
on keeping left at Shrewsbury. It was then
you became a slave to weather forecasts,
hoping to avoid the worst of it by hoping.

North Wales demanded the best water-proofs,
not the dusty winkle-pickers in Humphreys'
Penhryn shop where I found the suedes.
Shuffling and foraging for two that matched
she laughed when I offered her a cheque.

I needed to stop but as we might've made it
to Burnley I held on. Though sensible,
the shoes were about as comfortable
as football boots to drive in and by the time
I'd become desperate the weather was too.

A wet start then. Your laughter felt like
a change of weather but then the wind
changed too and I was pissing into it.
Driving south in soiled shoes and groping
for an image, I'd miss the football.

IN THE MOOD

From a story told by Spike Milligan
about the funeral of Peter Sellers.

Drowning syncopation with applause,
they giggled and played along
with the early bars of his last request,
knowing he'd hated the song.

Somehow, since he knew they'd know,
it seemed a way to mark the divide,
a rush of blood they might be excused
mistaking for death's funny side.

But anyone who's ever played the fool
in a cemetery needs no persuasion:
the one consolation a Fool sees through
is the haunting, on this occasion
making them shudder irresponsibly
at the grave, suppressing laughter.

WOMAN IN A SEDAN

John Keats: Letter to Tom,
                    9th July, 1818.

In the worst of kennels she squats in state,
the Duchess of Dunghill, like an ape
starved of biscuit on the way
from Madagascar to the Cape.

An Irish mile is half as much again
in English, and twice the cost
when you're bumped along
by ragged girls in a place you've lost.

Try to imagine her life and sensations.
Squab and lean but slave to a pipe
and puffing like a Scotch cottage,
she drags her head from side to side.

SCHOOL SONG

Each for another's and none for his own!

The men have abandoned their rags and paint
in something resembling a hurry,
but the boys still strain to be a choir.

After gathering himself in busy whispers
a monk had shimmered past them
and slid through the wall, disappearing

down corridors left half-creamed
beyond the renovated hall
and Elizabethan stucco facades.

But only to re-appear later perusing
a few names we scratched here.
He must have drifted away again

in search of old selves, maybe unaware
that even spirits have to line up
in single file with the rest.

Would Simms have welcomed this new face
with the usual ceremony:
Be seated, both hands on the book,

or Willy have stood there patting his
tweed pocket for the challenge:
Is it heads or tails, big boy?

Would he be given the shorter shrift
by Charlie, whose Latin
came spiced with U.F.O. pap,

or Lenny, a good inch under five foot
and boasting perfect pitch
to scare us into song?

Surely he'd have sung out of habit,
having no need of miming
last lines or yelling the refrain.

Or did he vanish to avoid other ghosts?
Here's one now, centuries
dimmer and less likely to surprise,

one who seems hooked on remembering
lines to a muffled hymn
and sizing up the front elevation.

There's a kind of purpose in its glare
until it sidles away
self-consciously and takes a fade —

like one of history's bloodless anecdotes
thrown back. It Pauses
only to glance at a standard letter.

The buff package insists it is not a circular,
is crammed with old boys'
destinations and a list of leavers' prizes:

Dear *Forth*, it says, we are pleased
to inform you. The hardback
*Dream Interpretation*s I think it was.

IN THE DESERT

The sky hangs low, in troublesome
haze, being watched.
The hills are watching each other.

Memorials sizzle and contract.
A mindful generation loiters,
taking in the sights,

and a small boy fills his water-pistol.
Troopers hoist him from the well
to his perch on the shield of a jeep

where he steadies to aim. He's careful
enough for a game of squirting
the corporal's trigger-finger.

Relaxed in the heat of afternoon,
they laugh when their faces are wetted
with each near miss, then stiffen

to level their eyes at the usual
bus-load. A mile and a half
from Bethlehem, we need a guard.

LEAVING JERUSALEM

Cicadas loud as planes
have been gathering since dawn
at the city's edge,
the hotels uncoiling early
with pickled eggs
and the newspaper war.

Two hours on, the last bus
strikes south into
gulleys and midday heat,
burning its reflection
back into the hills.
We sit in the upholstery

and wait in vain for a breeze,
dozing until a man
blunders into the aisle
and waves an arm
towards the bell-push,
catching the driver's eye.

Gears and automatic doors
bump into neutral
and we stop in a cloud,
all eyes on him as he floats
on haze and disappears
into sand. The engine coughs

and fires when we pull away,
drowning to a buzz
in seconds. The earth
turns and fries its bones,
bleached and drowsy
for the Feast of Spring.

THE BULL GAMES

I

We can almost taste waves when our wheels swing under
and the comforting flaps move in to shift spray.
A burned-out Stuka squats by a dis-used path
and the island tilts disconcertingly.

Zeus and *Hertz* For-Hire signs shimmer in the calm,
and Summer restores the glint of a dozen cars
buried when the hill came down.

As if in gratitude, finding them empty,
a couple of JCB's are lifting and lazily shoving
a mountain closer to the sea.

II

These footless walkers preserved in a busy arcade
look soft and stunning: women dressed in white
and the men in red have been jigsawed
into procession around the room.

We move at a healthier pace from town to ruin,
and two godlike eyes in the hill's face
follow us down, imagined through haze.

Above them the radar-scanners are watching
only sky, but our driver's cautious
even in pure weather. He chain-smokes,
repeatedly crossing himself
as we pass from below like a train.

III

The engineers drawing and masons hammering a throne
for High Priest Minos were barely a room away
from his seat as King, and landscapers
must have planned this backdrop for the pious.
All would burn their way to the altar,
their palms half-lifted in prayer,
earth-worn, clean and foetal as the grave.

We stand looking over a slope beyond the Horn
of Consecration, its cavity now built up
like an empty tooth with two-thirds crowned.
Pasiphae's stream-lined privy still looks
flimsy beside her boy, but her plans
to extend and replenish the frescoes
were almost complete when the earthquake came.

IV

Earlier marauders managed a few inroads,
stealing the trees in various wars
before being floated away.
Their rumours were never enough
to shake a palace hewn from the sand.

A relief-map good enough for selling
Island Cruises flaps below us
and the air-liner's buoyancy
feels like approaching sleep.

We ascend in circles chattering,
idly reading of new chambers to feed a feast
and the ritual shaving of young bone,
of how the gods were satisfied
and people expected only a quiet burial
in their baths at thirty-five.

PUBLICATION DAY

For Herbert Lomas

Just off a steamer and three days'
boozing your way through wet,
you settle down in the light
and tease some land-locked friends
held by your glittering eye.

You say you'd feel a bit queasy
if you were the only one here
still keen on God, that imagining
anti-Hell will do for now. The sea's
no habitation though we're drawn

by the icy flows and stay past twelve.
Outside, the quiet of a cliff
edge and nothing's mystery.
Inside, the air feels sharp
and nifty as a pack of sparrows.

ANTE-NATAL

Hospitals are best if you go for birth
head-on; they treat you better
if you play at being well
or belonging. Just for a moment

your recovery's tied to an intercom's
submarine blip and pleading,
and you warm to the echoes
of tricky soundings still to come.

In the picture at last and watching
the future at one remove,
you feel displaced or eased
to one side, apparently cured.

Baby's heart bobs like a floating nut
on a screen at seven months
and you're hooked already,
encouraged by the early kick or cry.

MOVING HOUSE

For Lizzie, aged one

Not being's clearer than being elsewhere
and exile hid your *SOLD* sign's
clarity from others only,
but what could you know of the home
you were shuffled into?

Before you'd taken your first steps
we'd left its overbearing blooms
and burned a ton of roses here
where trees dropped sour apples
and memories couldn't reach you.

We tried to stop you eating them
but the odd one or two slipped through.
You were given away by the mime
of secrecy and poor appetite
when we were learning your ways.

Your quick-slow adjustment of pace
to the slope of an angled house
leaves everything to chance.
Make your way down to us
tonight, and we'll try that dance.

AN OUTLOOK

Future rebels could've swung these beams
or dashed with their troublesome mates
to laugh at the stocks, and the church's

almost unique little fish-eye window
glimpses graves. All houses descend
from the land with their biscuit frontage.

With one door for tinkers and the King's men
we'll not have housed the rich.
The boards still creak like musket-shot.

None of our curtains or matting match
stone-mullion's rough round edges,
but the Town Council Planning Commission

for controlling listed buildings (grade II)
will consider one half-metre skylight
knocked, with care, through local history.

FISH-KILLS

Someone I knew with a streamlined
pond had pumps and runnels
purified, newly licensed for trout.

War-like forms would shimmy into view,
recalling my Nan's bloaters
and their sharpened, smoky tang.

Our children stood at the edge, cooing
and launching crumbs, thrilled
with each delicately poised attack

and a life glimpsed on the water-line.
But it's the whiff of sweet suppers
gives this aftermath its glare,

though death is nothing stiff to a fish
whose tiny intermittent flap
is the ultimate feigning.

Deep in purpose-built splendour,
clogged weeds are waving
their missiles as we take tea.

Later, your sprats on the slab
seemed like a poor attempt to kid us,
the years they've taken to fry.

We've nothing left but the new
crisp skins and a kitchen
full of brittle, roaring 'goodness'.

Our daughter counts and doles them out
for three, on the tray
of her gutted baby chair,

then holds one up. I love a little
fish, she says, blooding her
little finger in its one dead eye.

TRANSLATIONS

For Lizzie & Rosie

First Holiday

Anything but romantic, the sea was rough
and smelly for your induction,
making us lean closer than we thought.

Trips by land were worse, jolting and often
laboured in a faulty pram, your make-do
monogrammed sun-hat setting you apart.

When those merry-go-round-fronted
ferries hooted, sparkling in the distance,
you kicked and spluttered, still smiling
through it all except the city museum's

dark and simulated womb, its ten times
magnified foetus and amplified heart.
There your face shut down like a busy
fairground gone to lunch and slept it out.

Fifteen Months

One morning's intermittent staring into
the fishbowl and you're floundering.
Limp as a fish you fend off water,
plant one or two aimless consonants
and leave us behind. We stand looking
as high, dry and redundant as the cup
we offer — and feel your quick heart's
wheels grinding into quiet. You must be
taking on the strain of gauging
another depth — your breath's heavier
intake and tiny whistle becoming
a lull that feels like lift. We look in
and find you stranded, just witness
a last lunge as it whisks you into sleep.

Nineteen Eighty-three

Your palms out-stretched and tearful clamour
calls us back to the cot-bars
and we try to hush your mimicry and cries.
Some birds have tucked themselves in the eaves
for summer where they plead like babies
unharmoniously. Come morning,
the planes will again be rocking you awake
and perfecting a scream in the haze,
pretending their wars are with us always.

You'll cram fingers in each ear and wince
at the meaningless clash of wings
and we'll join you, inching closer
in a flock before the wheels, trying
not to hear the juggernaut circling our beds.

Translations

Fresh from clattering through woods
with your fists full of crumbs
you're sleeping fitfully,
and though the owl has given way
to cooing by your window,
we know you'll be awake too soon.

Freezing to the touch under covers
between us, you'll refuse
to be taken in; owls are known
for their mimicry of pigeon-sound.
You'll offer a new rendering
of bells: *Go! Go! Go!* repeatedly.

Later we'll search again for birds
squeezed thin by little secrets.

Wildlife Park

A dead chick fingered aside is unconvincing
and the hawks look tame with their chains
rivetted to boulders, but your bird-scaring
falters on the possibility of a landslide.

A child-sized monkey stops dissecting mice
to stare from its cage as we pass,
and you tell us we're eaten each night
by the house. We let ourselves be nagged

into shoulder-rides, once around the trail
and back, but your stilted talk in the car
proves we've left you there transfixed
by the keeper's jangling keys. We're taking
the longer way home to your dragons,
squat in the garden like heaps of loam.

A Walk By The River

For Jane and Elizabeth

The children bounced up and whispered
to a stranded pike, hot and grey
with its sprung teeth shielded
like feminine screw-thread.
They pattered and sniffed at the dry air
and dark sky gathering, poised for
the coming flood, and you were splayed
(as the fashion was) trying to take
a professional snap. Your dress took
your shape like a dancer's in the drumming
rain as we were running, and the wood
was filled with voices calling for shelter,
half-heartedly. Their party-piece ended
with drops being gathered as they fell.

Babies

When Cocky croaked and swung
pipe down you left me,
sick inside with a coat of red ice
forming on his former bowl.

The church bell's reliable gong
was saying first blood to us,
and the muddy corpse was surely
a sign of a kind of fight.

You cut him down and scuffled
leaves for a Winter fire,
fussing all day by the door
of the shed we left him in:
Now you're dead but don't you worry.
Let me kiss your claw.

Daughters

Another nightmare feels like this:
Come this way, said one old woman
and later, *Come with me,* another.
Their act of teasing me was waking you
as laughter gathered and grew.

Then your sister was suddenly running
from a grey-coated, drooling creature
as if life depended on it,
the one you'd earlier caught out
bloated on your friends but ready to listen.

Morning finds you relatively free
to pass on your own stories
with the marmalade: *Which only goes
to show how changeable men are.*

Seeds

You're caught foraging among dead lettuce,
in a setting made for talk of seed
and fertilisation with proper gravity,
trying for one that won't hurt the rabbit.
Just you three in a garden then —
your big, medium and little faces
getting to grips with love and down to cases.

Surely not *everyone*'s conceived that way?
Your struggle for the right ground's
within reach of one and beyond another,
who seems to be turning us all over
oblivious of anti-climax. Reared by people
who don't exist, she's bored anyway
if all's well and everyone survives the telling.

The Photos

Their nakedness makes you feel overdressed,
as when the farthest outcrop from shore
seems lit from close in, yet it raises
one more thing she needs to know:
you needn't answer if you don't know
(as if to prove logic's an indiscretion)
but if you don't, then just say so....

Sepia finish would have shut out the modern
discussion. It lumbered into life
much sooner, but *Kodachrome* clarity's
sharper focus betrays the bike
and rusty bell that couldn't be hers now,
proof only that she travelled when
she needed to, with no real glimpse of how.

CLOSE SHAVES

Staring yourself too long in the face
can trouble your belly like coming
down a slide too fast, too late —
as bad as going red from taking
chances on the razor-blade of love.

Back at the college unexpectedly
some years on and bearded
by one I'd known, or shaving
into my chin I can see a boy
in a backstreet Victorian school,

afraid of blemishes, needing a girl.
Or Jumbo torturing choirs
by dangling scales beyond their reach
and making his *cats chorus*
sing solo, backed by the laughter.

Down further, when elegant Miss Terry
hits her roof as *mum* slips out,
she cuts me clean as the coated sweet
for being immunised: If we'd only
keep still it wouldn't hurt a bit.

Sugar was all-pervading until your touch,
a hint of randomness on my hand.
I seem to have carried it back with me.
The rustling's a gathering of old souls
dreamily mooching home, downhill.

SOFT CLOCKS

How can we ever learn
to understand others,
their togetherness
together with the fact
they're not us,
said Dali to his beloved

Gala, who, recalling
his earlier vow
that if she died first
he'd eat her,
presumably checked her watch
when the moment came,

although not keeping to it
might've signified more
than ordinary words
or watches can measure,
luckily for others
and luckily for us.

TENTH ANNIVERSARY

Creuau, 1987

The bracken and walkways
have twisted to form
a knot by the lake,

a generous family portion
snug among heather
at the valley's crease.

We're overlooking
the grey church tucked in
like a sideshow

with its field of cattle
grazing one way,
suggesting more rain.

We stumble across
a leathery bat
that's hung itself to dry

in the slated barn.
The girls will gather
as they once did

for the smell of poached hare
in a gunslinger's bag,
reckoning blood

as water but redder.
Outside, their past is
what they'll miss.

Evening in the valley
hardly alters
for these migrations,

the darkness giving way
like a wary sea
to rattling stone,

but crowds of midges
feed on the mist
to make it feel like home.

Whatever we do tomorrow
we'd better hang on
to dry rock and climb.

NIL-ONE

i.m. J.G.

Liverpool had barely got going then
and we'd hung on for the draw up there
so it was odds-on with home form
we'd make it into the final rounds.

The crowds packed in like never again
and my brother stood on my feet for nearly
seventy minutes of trying to claw back
a narrow deficit and grab the extra-time

before remembering to ask me whether
I'd heard that John had died. It left me
with no grasp of the game, him having been
a fair player and younger than my dad.

YOUR GIFT FROM SOUTH AMERICA

Each passing bird's a cup of blood.
I eat what I've heard
and spit out the song,
growing in the heart
till I'm laid in a homespun hole.

Gathering life in the one dream,
I need no disease
when no speed escapes me.
I'm food for thought,
built like a bat on springs.

Keep me in a cool dry place
among those who won't
stare in too hard, too long.
Remember I'm never
the only one in the frame.

Expect a cruder awakening
whenever the dryness
signals my black prance.
I think I might be just
the thing to make you dance.

VICTORIANA

A Tale

When Grandmama first departed
and tight-lipped women
formed their tent of black
crinoline over her bed,

I lay pressed to my own
distracted by noise.
They were huddled in darkness
waiting for a sign.

How would they stifle
this terrible wail
like a struggle for birth
coming from the dead-room?

Some found reassurance
in my clinging to the counterpane,
of the soul's boundless
industry. She's going

in search of peace they said,
with only a friend's
bones for company.
They could feel her blessing

but none dared venture up to me.
Although she and I
had sworn to remain as foes
till Doomsday breaking,

we'd honour many a pact
and difficult promise
together in the haze
of each indifferent moon.

YOUTH

Even the house sits back in shadow
gathering rumour. Especially,
her uncle's hidden cache
in boarded tunnels under the floor
and how in the upstairs room
the sunlight clouds her eiderdown.

She'll not struggle up here again
to see her curtains faded
beyond repair, or a small girl
imposingly framed, beautiful
and forgotten clearly,
smiling like a hesitant star.

LAST ORDERS

One more drink and I'll be done.
We ain't as long 'ere as gone.
Don't ask why me ticker's wrong
when me throat's dry as a bun.

She's propping up my tottering herd
of sheep and goats on her table,
then posing for snaps like a new rebel
with a ten-gallon hat in the yard.

Just one more will turn me round.
Please God I never get old.
It's well past time you had me rolled
over and laid in the ground.

It's sunny but I'm kept from seeing
her new coffin shouldered out
a hundred yards away. They're saying
she drank money and did without

shoes, grub and schooling her kids,
try soothing me with a last
glance up the road and a promise
of Heaven I'm slow to grasp.

WATCHING BEES

They're measuring their steps again
to make a point, showing off
some peculiar taste then moving

as if they've been stung by light
and disappearing on a rumour.
Their disproportion makes any

landing hazardous, but they cling
to the pure chance in flight
and celebrate a kind of perfection.

Just watch them gathering any time
from all directions, dancing
whole days to a single blossom,

or listen to them burning up inside.
It's all they can do to get off
the ground. I'm circling closer

year by year, increasingly short
of air. The longer I watch
the less I believe in the honey.

CASTAWAYS

For Sylvia Kantaris

The best kind of company on an island
is someone unafraid of being an 'I'
(on the whole less likely to eat you,
or so you said), but the impersonality's

good for self-denial as well as tyranny,
and one for whom civilisation depends
on chopping the 'I' or passing the jam
could still dismantle an island's welfare.

Like the Cretan who insisted all Cretans
are liars, we could have it both ways
and try not to over-use the first person
or risk being insufficiently personal.

But sentimentality's a blight, it's true,
like harking back or needing a sail.
In these dislocated times, we Liberal
Humanists ought to stick together.

THE SIEVE

....who can say
what would have shaken from the sieve?

Wrapping up this book for the post
did not feel like letting a limb
go or giving birth or getting it back.

You might say moments of illumination
are outside time and, well....
illuminating, but you're downstairs

in the thick of it — and I've just spent
a morning looking at Yeats
with kids less than half my age

who took in *Words* and chucked it
back in tatters with no sweat,
as if he'd been dead these fifty years.

A FISHERMAN

Whatever you do don't talk fat.
No amount of clarity cuts any ice
when you're out of condition.
Nor will dieting help your voice
if it goes in lazy fits and starts.

Where I come from it's all strife;
most of the punters have a line
in plunder and gripe, still dripping
with Lord of the Manor's abuse.

I couldn't be doing with such a life
(choosing without any choice).
Here, where only thinner words
are news, I can make any fist I like
and raise it in a polite disguise.

TROUT

Live trout bare metallic teeth.
Dead, they'll bleed on a plate in the fridge,

revealing little crenellated jaws
and eyes that bubble in heat.

Such an end to elusive life
with twisted tails can be chilling;

to think of all that mythic power
winding up cooked with the head on.

Fish shouldn't really have any blood,
are never ripe for tickling.

DOOR TO DOOR

1587 - 1987

The hand-drawn map on our wall was snapped
by a lad from his find in the village crypt,
then mounted, framed and sold to us
cheap at the price. An Elizabethan forest,
tin-tacked in mushrooms over the heights,
looks cluttered with its shivering letters
and unfettered deer that preen themselves,
leap or are still. He says he'll be suing
the doctors who couldn't pluck his daughter,
eight weeks, from the jaws of a bad cold,
and we're looking intently at the map
as if to apologise. Its faded, unfurling
waters disappear off a yellowing
curled edge even older than the house.

CONCERTINA

August, 1939

This glossy village souvenir reveals
an eye for nostalgia — with lovers
posing unflustered in pre-war glaze.

Shown without their ring of black spikes
and creosoted finish, the stocks
look good enough to weather storms,

the graveyard's hidden by a bulky tree
and the monument's blown clean
for each November on parish funds.

Whole generations come to mind even now
when it's blasted. In those days
nearly everyone attended — half a band,

the young couple in the first few frames
and a dark-haired girl whose eyes
smoulder like the Angel's at Mons.

BROOCH

For Judy

Elgar's Birthplace, January 14th, 1991.

An authentic wind-up gramophone's on display
with half a dozen replacement pins,
the original dog is laid
to proper rest outside, and the antique
hats and coats are getting an airing.
Une Voix Dans Le Desert hangs
on a whitewashed wall
upstairs, and the man himself fills
all four rooms on clinical CD.

We've seen the desk and manuscripts,
the reading from *Boys Own Tales* to *Early Church*
our mums and dads remember,
his busy books of half-done squares
and a whole household of brisk Edwardian
Elgars passing without a smile.
The fiddle he sold for ten pounds-six
a hundred years ago brings back
the one I've been saving for your lapel.